# Kip and Wags

by Kristin Winters
illustrated by Laura Morgan

Practice Decodable 11

McGraw Hill Education

Bothell, WA • Chicago, IL • Columbus, OH • New York, NY

**MHEonline.com**



Send all inquiries to:
McGraw-Hill Education
8787 Orion Place
Columbus, OH 43240

ISBN: 978-0-02-144946-0
MHID: 0-02-144946-5

Printed in the United States of America.

8 9 10 CTM 23

Look at the cup.

It has milk for Kip.

Kip is a kid.

Look at the pan with milk.

It is for a cat, Wags.

Kip has milk with Wags.

Wind tips a cup.
Just Wags has milk!